CITY SHAPES

For Danny, Kate,
and Jane
— D.M.

To Haley, Chloe,
and Ava Collier
and all children who take
the time to observe
their world
— B.C.

The illustrations for
this book were done in watercolor
and collage on 400-pound Arches watercolor
paper. The text was set in Neutra Text PS, and the
display type is Roller World BTN. • This book was edited
by Allison Moore and designed by Roberta Pressel with art
direction by Saho Fujii.

ISBN 978-1-338-18521-8

12 11 10   20 21 22

Printed in the U.S.A.   40

First Scholastic printing, September 2017

Cover design by Saho Fujii
and Roberta Pressel

CITY SHAPES

By **Diana Murray**

Illustrated by **Bryan Collier**

SCHOLASTIC INC.

A pigeon takes flight through the bright cityscape,
exploring the scenery . . . **SHAPE** after **SHAPE**.

The city is bursting with **SHAPES** of each kind.
And if you look closely, who knows what you'll find!

A truck rumbling by
to deliver the mail,
a silvery cart with
hot pretzels for sale,

and stacks of brown
packages hauled up
the stairs . . .

Some **SHAPES** in the city are . . .

on-the-go **SQUARES.**

A skyscraper covered in shimmering glass,
a long metal bench near a green patch of grass,
and a table with glittery scarves and gold bangles . . .

Some **SHAPES**
in the city are . . .
dazzling
RECTANGLES.

The seaport with all of its flowing white sails,
and there, in the market, the pointy fish tails,
and colorful flags on a banner that dangles . . .

Some **SHAPES** in the city are . . .
gleaming **TRIANGLES.**

The sunglasses worn by a cop on his beat,
the wheels of the taxis that zip down the street,
and a manhole that leads to the pipes underground . . .

Some **SHAPES**
in the city are . . .
CIRCLES,
so round.

At sunset the city is softly aglow
as chitchatting crowds hustle-bustle below,
when off in the distance a melody hums.
It's hard not to follow the sound of the drums.

The stage in the park where the instruments sing—
some **SHAPES** in the city are . . .
OVALS that swing.

And nearby, the kites seem to dance in the sky.

Some **SHAPES** in the city are . . .
DIAMONDS that fly.

The sun fades away into
hazy blue dark,
and soon there's a twinkle,
a glimmer, a spark.

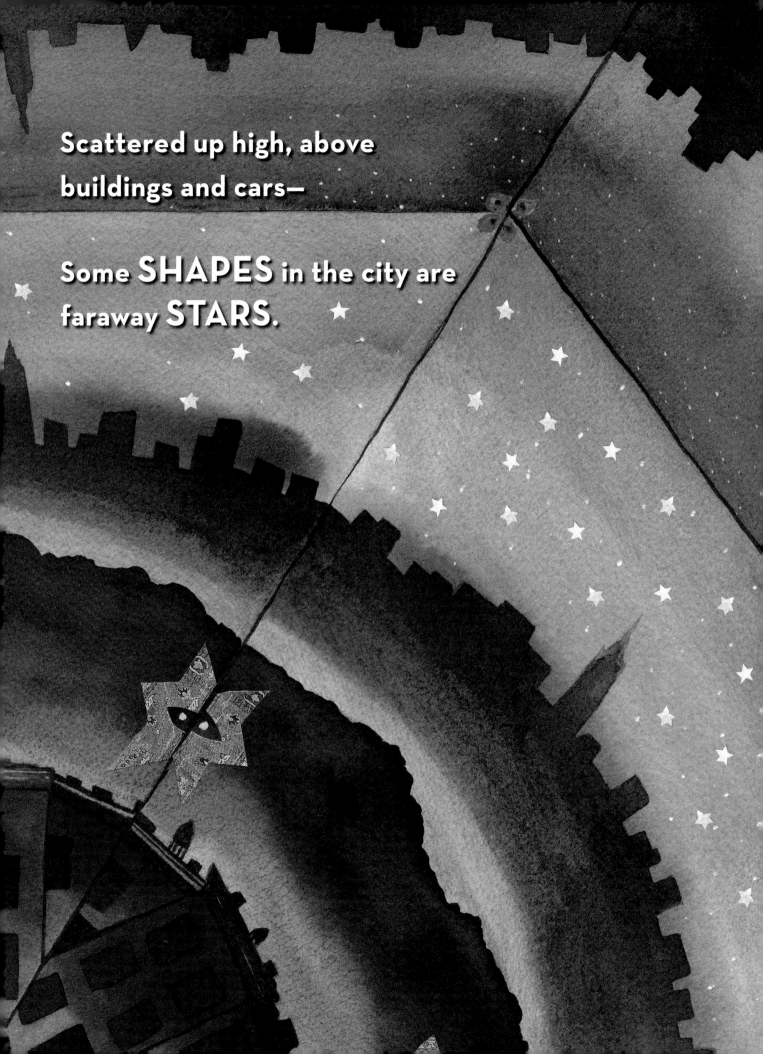

Scattered up high, above
buildings and cars—

Some **SHAPES** in the city are
faraway **STARS.**

The pigeon flies back through the night cityscape as city lights sparkle, SHAPE after SHAPE. But her heart starts to ache for the SHAPE she loves best. The SHAPE that is *home*—

her warm **CIRCLE** nest . . .

where the whirring and beeping of cars rushing by
helps her fall fast asleep, like a sweet lullaby.

AUTHOR'S NOTE

I was born in Ukraine and immigrated to New York City at the age of two. I lived in a tall building with a balcony that gave me a bird's-eye view of the neighborhood. Sometimes I even got to wave to my friend on a balcony across the street. For many years after college, I lived in busy midtown Manhattan, where parades regularly marched under my window and the familiar ebb and flow of city traffic lulled me to sleep each night.

On weekends, I often took a "hike" around the city (hiking boots and all!), walking for miles, all the way down to Chinatown and back again. I loved the way the neighborhoods changed, the diversity of the architecture, the people, and the interesting discoveries around every corner. That was my inspiration for writing this book. I recently moved to a nearby suburb with my two wonderful daughters and my husband, who is a New York City fire chief. It's fun to have my very own backyard, but whenever I go back to the city, it still feels like home.

Diana Murray

ARTIST'S NOTE

City Shapes is a wondrous journey of discovery through the eyes of our young tour guide as she shows off as much of her world as she can in the span of a full day. This little girl (who happens to be my four-year-old daughter) leads us throughout her neighborhood, urging us to notice things we hadn't spotted before: some shapes that we will recognize right away and some that require a closer look. Meanwhile, a bird flies above, reminding us that there's always another perspective to consider.

The art for this book was done in watercolor and collage on 400-pound Arches watercolor paper. I think collage works so well with this story because it illuminates all the smaller elements and shapes to form a whole picture. When I read this text for the first time, I was immediately inspired. In this kaleidoscope of colors and shapes, I hope you can almost hear and taste the sounds and smells of this vibrant and colorful city day. And as night falls and the stars come out, you'll see how city and nature combine in a gentle mix of new tones and shapes to discover.

City Shapes

By Diana Murray

Show off what you know about shapes!

In the boxes below, either draw the shape that's named,
or fill in the blanks to name the shape.

(Ask for help with the spelling if you need it!)

_ _ _ _ _ _

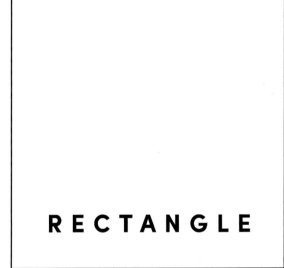

RECTANGLE

TRIANGLE

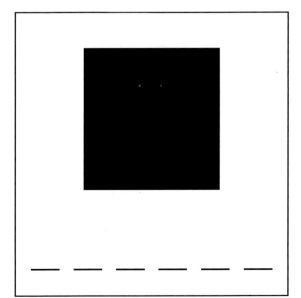

_ _ _ _ _ _ _

978-1-338-54454-1

SCHOLASTIC

City Shapes

By Diana Murray

Enjoy the Book Together

- There is so much going on in this book! After you read it together, go back and look at the different scenes. What's happening in each scene? What is everyone doing?

- The author uses interesting language to create the city for you. What words does she use to help you see, hear, smell, touch, and even taste the city?

Make Personal Connections

- How do you feel about cities? Do you live in one, or have you ever visited one? If not, would you like to? Why or why not?

- Look around right now, wherever you are! Can you find one example of each of the shapes in the book? Maybe you can even describe each one in a special way, like the author does!

Literacy Tip

Is this a book that tells a story, or a book that gives information? Actually, that's kind of a trick question—this book does both! It tells a story about a girl who lives in the city, but it also teaches about shapes.

978-1-338-54454-1